La Porte County Public Library
La Porte, Indiana

Are UFOs Real?

BY PATRICK PERISH

Amicus High Interest is published by Amicus
P.O. Box 1329, Mankato, MN 56002
www.amicuspublishing.us

Copyright © 2014 Amicus. International copyright reserved in
all countries. No part of this book may be reproduced in any
form without written permission from the publisher.

Library of Congress Cataloging-in-Publication Data
Perish, Patrick.
 Are UFOs real? / by Patrick Perish.
    pages cm. -- (Unexplained, what's the evidence?)
 Audience: K to grade 3.
 Summary: "Presents famous UFO sightings and briefly
examines the claims, some of which have no explanation and
some of which were hoaxes"-- Provided by publisher.
 Includes bibliographical references and index.
 ISBN 978-1-60753-386-3 (library binding) --
 ISBN 978-1-60753-434-1 (ebook)
 1. Unidentified flying objects--Juvenile literature. 2.
Unidentified flying objects--Sightings and encounters--Juvenile
literature. I. Title. II. Title: Are unidentified flying objects real?
 TL789.2.P47 2014
 001.942--dc23

                                 2012045079

Editor   Rebecca Glaser
Series Designer   Kathleen Petelinsek
Page production   Red Line Editorial, Inc.

Photo Credits
Shutterstock Images, cover, 21; Fernando Gregory/123RF,
4; 123RF, 7; Qasim, 8; Samuel Coccius, 11; Mary Evans
Picture Library/Alamy, 12; Elena Ray/Shutterstock Images,
14; Orhan Cam/Shutterstock Images, 17; Hector Mata/
AFP/Getty Images, 18; Igor Zhuravlov/123RF, 22; Digital
Vision/Thinkstock, 25; Yuriy Mazur/123RF, 26; M. Cornelius/
Shutterstock Images, 29

Printed in the United States of America at Corporate Graphics
in North Mankato, Minnesota.
5-2013 / P.O. 1152
10 9 8 7 6 5 4 3 2 1

Table of Contents

Some people say they have seen strange shapes in the sky.

 What other UFOs do people see?

What Are UFOs?

People see weird things in the sky. Sometimes it's a flash. Sometimes it's a fast flying shape. Every year hundreds of UFOs are reported. UFO stands for Unidentified Flying Object. The most famous UFOs are flying saucers.

 People see many shapes. Some see flying triangles, ovals, and squares. Others have seen tubes, balls, and even cones.

Many people think UFOs are **alien** spaceships. But UFOs are any unknown flying things. They could be airplanes. They could be meteors. But some are mysteries! Scientists study UFO reports. Some of them work with CUFOS. This is the Center for UFO Studies.

 Who else has studied UFOs?

UFOs might not be piloted by aliens. But they are unknown.

 The U.S. government studied UFOs. Its last official UFO program was Project Blue Book. It

Flying machines are mentioned in ancient writings.

First Reports

UFOs have been seen for thousands of years. The *Ramayana* is an ancient poem from India. It tells of flying machines called *vimanas*. They destroyed towns. Livy was a writer from ancient Rome. He wrote down strange **sightings**. Some people saw a flying boulder. Others saw flying shields and ships.

In 1561, UFOs appeared over Germany. They looked like tubes, crosses, and balls. They seemed to battle across the sky! Everyone was terrified. In 1566, UFOs were seen over Switzerland. Black balls filled the sky. They seemed to fight each other. Some seemed to catch on fire.

An artist drew this picture of the objects people saw in Switzerland.

11

Kenneth Arnold was flying his own plane when he saw UFOs.

 Were other UFOs seen in 1947?

The modern age of UFOs began June 24, 1947. Pilot Kenneth Arnold was flying over the Cascade Mountains in Washington. He was looking for a missing plane. He saw nine silver **crafts**. Zoom! They sped off. They flew much faster than planes. A reporter called them flying saucers. The name stuck. After that, many others reported UFOs.

A rancher in Roswell, New Mexico, found broken pieces of a UFO in his fields. The Air Force later said it was a weather balloon.

Some people have spotted
UFOs from their backyards.

 How do experts spot fake pictures?

UFO Reports: The Unexplained

In 1950, Evelyn Trent was outside her home in Oregon. She saw a flying saucer! She called to her husband. He got his camera. He took pictures of the UFO. Then it was gone. Experts have examined the pictures many times. The photos seem to be real.

Today, experts **scan** pictures into a computer. This lets them see things they couldn't before. They might see a wire holding up a UFO.

In 1952, **radar** picked up strange objects over Washington, DC. They hovered over the capitol. The Air Force was worried. They sent out fighter planes. But the UFOs disappeared! One pilot saw four bright lights. They flew away at amazing speeds. No one knows what these flying objects were.

Even the White House has had a UFO sighting.

Two men point to where
witnesses saw a UFO.

 Have lights like this been seen anywhere else?

The largest modern UFO sighting was March 13, 1997. That night, a triangle of lights glided over Phoenix, Arizona. They floated slowly above the trees. Thousands of people saw the lights. Some saw a spaceship. They said it was three football fields long! No one has been able to explain what happened.

 In 1951, people in Lubbock, Texas saw a triangle of lights. Experts have studied pictures taken of the lights. They are not false.

Exposing the Fakes

Some people *do* make up UFO stories. Dan and Grant Jaroslaw were brothers. In 1967, they took pictures of UFOs in their backyard. Their mom called the news. Experts couldn't explain it! Later the boys told the truth. The UFO was a **model**. They hung it on a string. The experts missed it. Before computers, spotting a fake was hard.

Some people have made
fake pictures of UFOs.

Many UFOs are tricks of nature. Clouds can look like flying saucers. Sun dogs are fake suns. They are **reflections** off ice crystals in the air. Sun pillars are, too. They look like long streaks. Meteors come in many colors. Rare lightning can look like ribbons or balls. Nature can play strange tricks!

Asteroids can look like spaceships.

Weird patterns have shown up in fields. They are called crop circles. The crops are flattened in a ring. Others are stars or spirals. Some say UFOs land in fields and make the shapes. In 1991, two men from England came forward. They said they made many of the crop circles. They faked them for thirteen years! But crop circles in other places have not been explained.

 How did the men make crop circles?

Crop circles have appeared in many places.

 They wore shoes tied to planks. They put a stick in the ground and tied a rope to it. They walked around and around. This made a perfect circle.

Alien ships would have to travel to Earth from far-off planets.

What's the Evidence?

Most UFOs aren't likely to be alien ships. Aliens would have to travel from planets outside our solar system, **light-years** away. Some people think UFOs are secret government planes. Others say they are caused by nature. **Witnesses** and photos give proof. But eyes can be tricked. Fake photos can fool even experts sometimes.

Each year, hundreds of UFOs are reported. Many can be explained, but some cannot. Scientists are always learning, though. Maybe someday they'll solve the mystery. Until then, we can only wonder. What do you think?

 How many people believe in UFOs?

There are many explanations for UFOs.

 A 2007 poll showed 34% of Americans believe in UFOs and 14% said they've seen one.

Glossary

alien A living creature from another planet.

craft A vehicle that can fly in air or in outer space.

light-year The distance light travels in a year, about 5,878,630 million miles (9,460,730 million km).

model A small, man-made version of a larger object.

radar A machine that uses radio waves to find solid objects.

reflection An image of something that is bounced off an object.

scan To examine or copy an image or document using a machine.

sighting The act of seeing something.

witness A person who saw or heard something firsthand.

Read More

Burgan, Michael. *Searching for UFOs, Aliens, and Men in Black.* Mankato, Minn.: Capstone Press, 2011.

Halls, Kelly Milner. *Alien Investigation: Searching for the Truth about UFOs and Aliens.* Minneapolis: Millbrook Press, 2012.

Polydoros, Lori. *Top 10 UFO and Alien Mysteries.* North Mankato, Minn.: Capstone Press, 2012.

Rooney, Anne. *UFOs and Aliens.* Mankato, Minn.: Smart Apple Media, 2010.

Websites

Chasing UFOs
http://channel.nationalgeographic.com/channel/chasing-ufos/

Crop Circle Secrets
http://www.cropcirclesecrets.org/

UFO Evidence
http://www.ufoevidence.org/

Index

About the Author

Patrick Perish spent many childhood nights under the covers with a flashlight and good book. In particular, aliens, ghosts, and other unexplained mysteries have always kept him up until the wee hours of the night. He lives in Minneapolis, MN where he writes and edits children's books.